FULL MOON OF AFRAID AND CRAVING

THE HUGH MacLENNAN POETRY SERIES

Editors: Allan Hepburn and Carolyn Smart

Waterglass Jeffery Donaldson

All the God-Sized Fruit Shawna Lemay

Chess Pieces David Solway

Giving My Body to Science Rachel Rose

The Asparagus Feast S.P. Zitner

The Thin Smoke of the Heart Tim Bowling

What Really Matters Thomas O'Grady

A Dream of Sulphur Aurian Haller

Credo Carmine Starnino

Her Festival Clothes Mavis Jones

The Afterlife of Trees Brian Bartlett

Before We Had Words S.P. Zitner

Bamboo Church Ricardo Sternberg

Franklin's Passage David Solway

The Ishtar Gate Diana Brebner

Hurt Thyself Andrew Steinmetz

The Silver Palace Restaurant Mark Abley

Wet Apples, White Blood Naomi Guttman

Palilalia Jeffery Donaldson

Mosaic Orpheus Peter Dale Scott

Cast from Bells Suzanne Hancock

Blindfold John Mikhail Asfour

Particles Michael Penny

A Lovely Gutting Robin Durnford

The Little Yellow House Heather Simeney MacLeod

Wavelengths of Your Song Eleonore Schönmaier

But for Now Gordon Johnston

Some Dance Ricardo Sternberg

Outside, Inside Michael Penny

The Winter Count Dilys Leman
Tablature Bruce Whiteman
Trio Sarah Tolmie
hook nancy viva davis halifax
Where We Live John Reibetanz
The Unlit Path Behind the House Margo Wheaton
Small Fires Kelly Norah Drukker
Knots Edward Carson
The Rules of the Kingdom Julie Paul
Dust Blown Side of the Journey Eleonore Schönmaier
slow war Benjamin Hertwig
The Art of Dying Sarah Tolmie
Short Histories of Light Aidan Chafe
On High Neil Surkan
Translating Air Kath MacLean
The Night Chorus Harold Hoefle
Look Here Look Away Look Again Edward Carson
Delivering the News Thomas O'Grady
Grotesque Tenderness Daniel Cowper
Rail Miranda Pearson
Ganymede's Dog John Emil Vincent
The Danger Model Madelaine Caritas Longman
A Different Wolf Deborah-Anne Tunney
rushes from the river disappointment stephanie roberts
A House in Memory David Helwig
Side Effects May Include Strangers Dominik Parisien
Check Sarah Tolmie
The Milk of Amnesia Danielle Janess
Field Guide to the Lost Flower of Crete Eleonore
    Schönmaier
Unbound Gabrielle McIntire
Ripping down half the trees Evan J
whereabouts Edward Carson

The Tantramar Re-Vision Kevin Irie
Earth Words: Conversing with Three Sages John Reibetanz
Vlarf Jason Camlot
Unbecoming Neil Surkan
Bitter in the Belly John Emil Vincent
unfinishing Brian Henderson
Nuclear Family Jean Van Loon
Full Moon of Afraid and Craving Melanie Power

Full Moon of Afraid
and Craving

MELANIE POWER

McGill-Queen's University Press

Montreal & Kingston • London • Chicago

ISBN 978-0-2280-1106-4 (paper)
ISBN 978-0-2280-1338-9 (ePDF)
ISBN 978-0-2280-1339-6 (ePUB)

Legal deposit second quarter 2022
Bibliothèque nationale du Québec

Printed in Canada on acid-free paper that is 100% ancient forest free
(100% post-consumer recycled), processed chlorine free

We acknowledge the support of the Canada Council for the Arts.

Nous remercions le Conseil des arts du Canada de son soutien.

Library and Archives Canada Cataloguing in Publication

Title: Full moon of afraid and craving / Melanie Power.

Names: Power, Melanie (Author of Full moon of afraid and craving),
   author.

Series: Hugh MacLennan poetry series.

Description: Series statement: The Hugh MacLennan poetry series |
   Poems.

Identifiers: Canadiana (print) 20220132682 | Canadiana (ebook)
   20220132739 | ISBN 9780228011064 (softcover) |
   ISBN 9780228013389 (PDF) | ISBN 9780228013396 (ePUB)

Classification: LCC PS8631.O8395 F85 2022 | DDC C811/.6—dc23

This book was typeset by Marquis Interscript in 9.5/13 Sabon.

CONTENTS

Ode to McCain's Deep'n Delicious Cake 3
The Real Pleiades 6
Your Past Selves Attend Your Birthday Party 9
Basel Penpal 11
Ode to Great-Uncle Will's Shine 14
Light of a Fractured Moon 16
After Apple-Picking 19
If You Answer Yes to Any of the Following Questions 21
Elegy to 17 22
After Midnight 23
Ode to the ½ Moon 25
Antigonish at Dawn 29
it hurt to be nowhere 31
Magic Show 33
I Should Have Guessed 35
Names like quartz in the mouth 36
Harvest 37
Picking Season 38
Across the Marshes 41
archipelago 43
Ode to Tunnock's Caramel Log 45
Frost in October 48
Roman Aubade 50
Ode to Sleep 51
sfogliatella 53
Elegy for the Linden Tree 56
Iceberg in Ferryland 57
Power's Store 59
My Father's Father 61

I have not always been as careful as I am now   64
The Fever and the Fret
  I. Rue Garnier   65
  II. Avenue Querbes   70
  III. Avenue St-Marc   72
  IV. Rue Clark   73
  V. Rue Saint-Dominique   76
  VI. Avenue de Normanville   81
I come home to remember why I have to leave again   91
Shaar Hashomayim Cemetery   92
Andromeda   94
the stone   95
Purple Balloons   97

Notes   101
Acknowledgments   103

FULL MOON OF AFRAID AND CRAVING

At twenty-six ingredients, it's engineered as intricately
   as a vehicle, with twice the alchemic intrigue.

From the ashes of yer youth, it rises up
   plastic-domed, perfectly preserved, on sale

two for one. In saccharine worship, your mouth
   still waters, that synthetic vanilla potent,

the way imitation of a thing in nature inevitably
   becomes overdone, but the garnish – delicate

chocolate tendrils – epitomizes refinery. A marvel
   of twentieth century technology, the frozen cake defies

time. Stretching the life of foods like
   the Sorcerer's Stone for wizards would,

freezers first entered Calvert kitchens
   in 1950-something. If we began then

to live less in the moment, at least fewer
   of my cousins went to bed hungry.

The O'Tooles on The Point bought one
   of the earliest fridges off analogue Kijiji –

just Steve Maddox driving up the shore,
   reselling goods from Fort Pepperrell out

the back of his trunk. Anyone who claims
   Canadian cuisine is non-existent hasn't

heard of McCain, born & raised in
   New Brunswick, the world's largest

retailer of frozen potatoes. Spuds for
   the Powers are like a good Burgundy

for the French: no meal was complete
   without them, and dessert was best

served from the freezer. On birthdays,
   a Deep'n Delicious was discharged from

frigid storage, and a sibling's leftover candles
   shoved into it. You watched as yer childhood

receded like a coastline as the candles
   annually gave off more heat. We shifted

our faith in the nineties to scientists from
   bakers, because we loved the uniformity

of stiff, factory-piped icing, because his mother's
   been gone so long my Dad almost forgets

how her homemade bread smeared
   with fresh cream & molasses tasted.

Wouldn't Mary-Essie have loved
   something ready-made, something

she could buy to trade for time? Unlike
  fallible French pastry, which ages every

sixty seconds and by day two isn't fit
  to bite into, one of these bad boys

maintains its integrity into infinity (or,
  for around six months, which is

as much of the future as is safe to
  bet on) Visit your local grocery store!

This frozen cake, at its rim, waits
  under fluorescents for you to carry

it home. *Do not heat or bake. Just thaw,
  cut, and serve.* Nothing gold can stay?

Robert Frost never tried
  a Deep'n Delicious cake.

In our diary lines, they lived
  their most epic lives. Nick, Dave,

Brad, Tim, monosyllabic gods
  smattered with acne. Their desire

like cirrus clouds stretched over
  classrooms, plunging us into shadow.

Leah kept the paper towel
  Josh wiped his muddy shoe in,

while Sarah scrawled in Hilroys,
  imagining her surname as Justin's.

The smell of post-hockey hair was
  its own semiotics of godly,

and that locker-room gossip urgent &
  opaque to us as Delphic prophecies.

With the hours Laura-Lee spent decoding
  Brian's messages, she could've picked up

Spanish or German. Against their bravado,
  we modulated the pitch of our songs, honing

the art of being watched. Without need for
  speech, Angie lent Ashley a sweater

to cover the blood splotch on her jeans.
  We stuffed lunches into bedroom

garbage cans, counted a cup of coffee's calories,
  transmitted eating disorders to each other

like airborne diseases. Murray rolled blunts
  thick as torches, with hands that ticked

the seconds & minutes of our hearts, as
  we seesawed from Appear Offline to Online

to solicit a *sup?* from him. Some rose
  to almost every occasion, even

when uninvited – vigils under desks for
  Ms Smith's rose-scented neck, the mere

suggestion of breasts beneath Stephanie's
  Gap sweater. Our private opals

of desire – swelling pearls, or quartz
  behind tissue-stuffed bras. At Booth dances,

arms encircled shoulders while eyes
  shifted, love at the price of its indistinct

edges. Except Paul, an artist – he was
  so sensitive. Steven, too, whose

Axe Body Spray in 2005 perfumed every
  centre-city bedroom. He taught Kayla

to drive in abandoned lots with
   his pick-up in park. Our bodies

were a city we hoped would one
   day be familiar enough to visit.

Your eyes now weather the rainy sting
   of hindsight: all those diary pages

wrongly dedicated, your pen mislaying
   a hundred ways to call them

beautiful: your stellar friends, the real
   Pleiades. Glittering kin of Lip Smackers

and laughing, their nightly landline calls
   were electric light against the darkness.

YOUR PAST SELVES ATTEND
YOUR BIRTHDAY PARTY

And they are terrible guests. Look, they ate
   the last slice of tarte tatin! Of course

they didn't think to bring anything. Or else
   they bring dep wine and a bag of Lay's.

Their twenty-something toes stub errant
   couch legs, steps heavy enough

to dent hardwood, their sole intent surely
   to disturb each sleeping tenant below.

In the sink, they let crystal lowballs
   stack while drinking whiskey from

a mug, irreverent as always toward
   an object's intended purpose.

They mistake friends for therapists,
   professors for friends. They love too

many men named Steve. Way too fucking
   many. *Petition to end the name,* you joke, but

they don't get it. Elevated humour goes
   right over their twenty-something heads,

yet no one at the party seems to
   find you as hilarious as them.

They think buying a bed frame is equivalent
　　to settling down; they extol the perks

of sleeping directly on the ground. Being flawless,
　　they are ruthless with others' poor choices,

giving advice in shades of black & white. For
　　them, "cancer" still has potential as a metaphor,

and "death" is just one of the many lovely
　　literary themes in Joyce's "The Dead."

Leaving rooms and conversations without
　　segue or notice, every transition of theirs

is perfectly artless. But can't they see
　　how far you've come? After all, it was

your body that rented to them their ephemeral
　　lives. But they don't hear a word you say over

polemical opinions, those oft-recited stories,
　　that deep-seated fear of being boring.

Though you still adore the way they leave
　　parties. There one goes, subtle as fireworks:

stumbling through the door without bidding
　　a single goodbye, cigarette lit before crossing

the porch, tumbling into the dark, happy
　　to pocket the night and call it hers alone.

You were from a country known
   for its fondue, Lindt, white mountains.

They're called The Alps, you wrote. I could only
   respond: *Where I come from is really foggy and boring.*

We wrote, clicked send, did it again,
   turning my basement bedroom computer

into what I guess a cathedral for a believer is.
   We straddled two centuries, switching between

keyboard and pen. Online was a place I could go
   to not be alone. In one letter, you knocked back

Mythos at a hotel lobby in Corfu, sixteen being
   Europe's legal drinking age. *Wow,*

I wrote, *that's what freedom is.* I wasn't
   dissuaded that we had never spoken

face to face, having met online in '05 over
   a shared love of Morrissey on Myspace.

You said *Lucky Strikes are divine*, but all I had
   were rollies from my mom's bathrobe pocket.

Throughout my high school Europe trip,
   I was sure I'd bump into you –

as if a continent were the mall,
   and I'd spot you at the food court

sipping fountain Fanta from a straw.
   In the polaroid I posted to you that summer,

the sun filtered through a sinking city to land
   in lacey patterns upon the fancy boats. *They're called*

gondolas, you wrote. You saw Belle & Sebastian
   live in Zürich, cried to "Still Ill" in Paris,

while I skirted mosh pits at a handful
   of Riverdale punk shows. On my school trip,

we visited Murano's glass-blowing factory,
   sand & soda ash blown as thin as pages

that longed, it seemed, to be broken
   and mourned over. *Better broke than*

whole, you wrote. *Better to miss than to hold*.
   I could have kissed your fatalistic tone.

I stole the image of light hitting the factory
   window then, to put in a poem. We wrote, hit send,

did it again – for a year, until you stopped
   responding after you got a real-life girlfriend.

You said *she's a feminist*, but I didn't know what
    the word meant. In another message before it ended,

you wrote, *Your heart will drop at the gold mosaics*
    of Saint Mark's Basilica, but instead I got

pick-pocketed beneath the cross,
    looking for where the mosaic was.

I was missing home badly, or rather,
    my dog, but in the pew I stopped and I

closed my eyes and let the good
    of God roll over me –

I thought that in my reply
    to you, it was best to remove

the part about getting robbed
    and missing my dog but keep

that deep-sounding
    bit on God in.

Without colour or odour, it glistened
  with the healing promise of holy water.

'Twas a liquid pilgrimage to Lourdes
  from the shore at a saintly discount.

'Twas a fine way to wet your tongue after
  a hard ol' day at jigging had your body worn out.

Concocted under Will's sink, poured into
  glass bottles and occasionally imbibed by boys

far under the legal age to drink, it was a special
  recipe to circumvent Crown Law & poverty.

Time has yet to efface the dirt
  the shine left on their knees,

when they got too drunk to talk or walk. But
  that fun is beyond words; on such topics

my uncles are only winks & laughs & nods.
  Drunk is a secret you keep with the world.

What is it about booze that gets you closer
  to God than Sunday School ever does?

It is painful to be ordinary. Some nights you
  drink, and drink, and drink, searching

the desert for a better version of yourself.
   Some nights you chance upon the famed

Bethlehem stable, only to awaken
   the next day in yer shed, parched.

I don't know what kind of man Will was.
   All I know is Will married Till and they raised

Joe over on The Cross. In my eyes, Will Boland
   will always be the great maker of shine.

Such liquor has not lost its potency, distilled
   across decades, handed down as memory.

I myself longed for a different kind
   of legacy. Will, are you watching?

I can write in a straight line.

Before I was old enough to choose,
    it was an obligation to go. St Patrick's pews

offered stacks of the same book, one that
    was musty, boring. A kid on my street

persisted that *Santa and God are totally
    phony*. Mother Mary's body bent,

frozen in maudlin poses, cheeks slick
    with tears of glue. Her saucer eyes

stained our insides. She bore the son
    of God but doesn't know how hard it is

to mother daughters, their feet denting sand
    in Jerusalem – by puberty, they're cat-called.

The kid in the pew ahead was allowed
    to eat Fruit Roll-Ups throughout mass,

while I was bred on the penance. I knew
    what the world was because I saw it

in a Geography textbook once. Are you there,
    God? Like Jesus, this poem's speaker

was immaculately conceived. On
    his birthday, my sister & I always got

twice the gifts, divorce the miracle that
  doubles Christmas. Subtract the father,

the son, and the family is a holy ghost,
  but you can always add starch

or strangers to thicken dinner's gravy again.
  Joint custody is a car straddling

two spots in the parking lot, until fumes
  are the love of exhaust, and home is

the tide – an empty, endlessly fulfilling
  gesture. I never saw a moon that was full,

the light of a fractured one became
  enough for me to read a face by.

When St John's sleeps, you see
  grown men, women, even saints

like Francis crying. Which saint was it
  again, the one supposed to look

after the children? I took to the night
  like a hermit crab nestles into shell,

because the secrets adults buried
  I longed to tell / tell / tell. I left

myself, muted my heart, hid in
  the mind – learned the trick for turning

seagull to dove, casting water into wine.
  Throughout mass, the other children

claw and clutch at chests, pulling
  on nipples like drain plugs to liberate

a drink. Who wants a snack
  from a can? Just add water. I grew

six feet tall on formula food.

AFTER APPLE-PICKING

On Saturday mornings, the night before
 is smudged under your eyelids, makeup in
shades of bruises. Pepto-Bismol's pink milk cools

the acid that chews and broils
 your insides. Some people come here
for the apples, some for the photos.

We pull out our rusty French for township locals
 like we are back in junior high, passing notes
under desks, perpetually learning passé composé.

The past, it seems, can be an event ongoing
 or an event complete. Working nights as a busser
means it's been months since you saw the sky this early –

at which point, you ask, did I start loving
 mornings? The chill of another autumn
in the air, and some feeling I've outgrown.

At which point does the way
 we know someone become a coat
that no longer keeps them warm?

It feels antique to be out of the city,
 picking our own McIntosh, Lobo, Gala,
Spartan. The way we laugh is a well-worn path.

We climb the ladders to orchestrate candid poses,
    lying later in a row of Cortlands, thumbing
our phones. Sneaking sweet bites, we post photos

to our feeds to harvest the likes. On the tractor ride,
    we are interlopers amongst honeyed couples, their
model kids. Your eyes roll at my routine bitterness.

Before driving back, you sampled every cider in eyeshot
    of my fledgling sobriety. The city we grew up in was
small as an orchard, wide as its own country.

The apples we got lasted long after we stopped
    talking. To spare them from rot, I converted
pounds of them into jars of frozen applesauce.

IF YOU ANSWER YES TO ANY
OF THE FOLLOWING QUESTIONS

Do all of your favourite protagonists end up alone? Was the inaugural heartbreak of your life not your own? Did you wait? Have you ever related to the moon? Do you know by heart, the statistics on marriages that end in divorce? Have you joked about them at engagement parties? Are you no longer being invited? Have you ever performed Patsy Cline at karaoke? Was the room totally empty? Do you avoid open bars and/ or buffets? Have you ever quoted the opening lines of *Anna Karenina* at a house party? Do you suffer from poor object constancy? Have you ever told an unsuspecting bartender your life story? Did you wait? Do you ever get emotional vertigo? Did you gift a copy of *Notes From Underground* to your first lover? Have you ever let down your guard to find there were a hundred guards behind it? Is "Please, Please, Please Let Me Get What I Want" your favourite Smiths song? Do you open your windows too soon after spring arrives, every time? Did you ever wait? When a woman held you too close, did you stay until she fell asleep, then leave her house? Have you ever suppressed a profession of love; was it like shackling a goldfinch, or letting it go? Are you, yourself, divorced? If so, how many times? Did you wait? Does the trope of the evil stepmother feel personal? Did you have an emo, punk, or goth phase? Did you wait? Did you? Did you ever wait to get picked up in a school parking lot until dark? Did you scream in an open field, or go round and still, like a stone.

For all the tight-jeaned, face-painted pleas to be pretty,
    God could drive up to my door
and take 17 right back from me.

Not a drop of sense in my head
    and each desire reducible to a slew
of tight-jeaned, face-painted pleas to be beautiful.

Five years since you sat in a pew, or
    ate a stale wafer at communion, you pray
for someone to take 17 back again.

In similar throes of girlhood, what would Jesus do? Pluck
    and wax, erase and trim – you want to be baby-new. You
whisper tight-jeaned, face-painted pleas to be beautiful.

Eyebrows don't quite grow back, but most hair
    rises on the third day, blacker – God could drive up
and take 17 right back from me.

Every anti-drug poster told you not to,
    so you start smoking for something to hold onto.
    For all the tight-jeaned, face-painted pleas
to be pretty, God could take 17 right back from me.

AFTER MIDNIGHT

The rain shifts to snow
  on The Main, streetlights

crowning flakes with foggy
  halos. In closed store alcoves,

lost teens imbibe covert swigs
  of gin, each gulp seems to hearten

them, dulling the wind that preys
  on inches of exposed skin. Later,

they'll crowd Plateau bar bathrooms,
  exchanging secrets. Pulling bullets

of lipstick from half-zipped
  backpacks, they withdraw caps

with a pop. They apply, then blot.
  Reapply, stifle laughter, blot:

the onomatopoeia of fake ID Fridays.
  When their favourite song comes on,

for three minutes, their problems
  unflower. Blossoming unafraid

onto sticky dancefloors, they sway
  in imagined wind, shielded by illusions

of safety that years & strange hands
   will not return to me. After midnight,

they'll droop, drunk tulips –
   too-soft stems with big, beautiful

heads. They wear unroofed love
   for each other in lieu of coats,

their trichomes are voltage as
   fingers touch. At last call,

they stumble out in vintage leather
   & jeans to anoint sidewalks with

cigarette smoke & fruity shampoos, bodies
   sardined now into a taxi's backseat.

Snow collects in clumps onto the roof
   of the car, a thousand flakes

of their divinations falling, falling
   from the sky onto the boulevard.

ODE TO THE ½ MOON

Vachon's ½ Moon
  is a pastry you could take

to deep space. Time or
  gravity cannot change

its perfect molecular composition,
  individually wrapped, ageless.

Chocolate or vanilla, it stays tender
  and moist forever, no, really,

did you ever see one go off?
  In 1923, the Vachon family

abandoned farming in Sainte-Marie
  to buy a bakery – eventually,

homemade cakes became
  industrially automated. Impervious

to mould, decay, these pastries will
  outlast most marriages, not excluding

yer parents'. If Catholics' faith in the church
  has waned, the ½ Moon rises in the same,

sacred arc-shape, but Mudder swears
  in the sixties they were bigger. At thirteen

in Witless Bay, she would steal out
   on lunch breaks to Howlett's Store,

her stinking fingers froze,
   trading her fish plant wage

for a Vachon cake. A quarter then
   was sovereignty, when it could still

get you a bun & tin of drink. We prefer
   the ½ Moon's ingredients a secret,

but if you must know, it is part
   cumulus cloud, part oxygen, part

edible pillow, yes, it is fitting that Kate
   finds them in her dreams, in which

we eat between swigs of Diet Pepsi.
   No need for nutritional facts, we know

the moon to rise and set calorie-free.
   The ½ Moon is conceived in a lab,

much like a baby is nowadays, and like
   a newborn's head, it is impressionable

to a hasty hand – indelicate fingers *will*
   indelibly dent it. Like Quality Street

candies, each family member has
   their favourite Vachon pastry:

Mudder wouldn't say no to a Billot Log,
   but her favourite is the Flakie.

Fabulous Foods over on Merrymeeting
   bakes one from scratch but at *that* price,

she prefers them freshly packaged
   from the factory, on sale at Sobeys.

Ian loves the Jos Louis, twin rose-brown
   cake rounds fused by a mortar of white icing.

Not sure if it was ever legal
   to sell them as singles,

but you could buy them that way
   at Red Circle on Dillon Crescent,

freed from their boxes, beside rows
   of Chubby Soda. In the early aughts,

the price of a ½ Moon on The Brow
   was just short of a loonie, when a loonie

meant golden autonomy. The crinkle
   of a Vachon wrapper in your pocket

was plastic happiness as you tore
   across concrete, dodging packs

of stray boys, their yapping jaws, your
   heart a full moon of afraid & craving,

always pushing your feet homeward
  like Atlantic tide toward the beach.

during that   violet summer
    of long rides   and holy Ford silence

annual boredom   of province-wide
    drives   along Route One   eyefuls

of balsam firs   the Ford puttered
    its path to the west coast

the way   my sister and I   knew best by
    roadway sugar stops   jacked on Fun Dip

and pop   we kept our peepers
    peeled for moose   or roadkill

the splatting of flies   on the windshield
    to add to the toll   playing rounds

of I Spy   singing Shania Twain for all
    510 miles   to Three Rock Cove

the third of its rocks   that signal its shore
    since whittled invisible   by waves

but the saltbox homes still   dot the coast
    plain lonely ghosts   my stepmother's

childhood home   is wood-fire warm
    the toast   bears the imprint of the stove

her parents back then   made a living
   from fishing   awake before dawn

they braved the bay   to comb the sea
   for crab and cod through sheets

of rain   drizzle   fog   last stop was
   Nova Scotia   didn't know then

it was my last family vacation   teenage years
   pine needles into skin   and even

in a crowded car   my body   floated
   alone   through all my car sleeps

it was while driving   through Antigonish
   at dawn   the car darkened   in spurts

as we wove through hills   and burst
   into light   as we exited a tunnel

jolted   awake   by the sound
   of dozens of birds pounding

the top of the Ford   in staccato thuds
   Dad pulled over   to floss their bodies

from the luggage racks   *They are not*
   dead   he said   *they are*

sleeping   and about that
   I still believe him

do you ever   do you remember how we
        performed odes   to crowds   of downtown

seagulls   who scoured sidewalks for
        stray fries or   the edible debris of

artists   a.k.a. people unlike us   w/ interesting lives
        we prowled alleys like   feral cats

with no homes   writing   Rimbaud on
        windshields of snow   getting dumb

on dive bar rum & cokes   penning each other
        love letters   with chokehold

promises && crooked verbs   yes   it was
        either yesterday   or   a decade ago

our legs locked   at awkward angles
        in the backseat of yer car   rocking   in empty

mall   or store or   church   parking lots   too awake
        we dreamed   of leaving the shell

it hurt to be nowhere   being seventeen
        we had no clue   what we were doing

but we had seen   a few Criterion movies
        it'd been months   since we broke up

when I called you   from a payphone
          said I needed a ride   said the night before

something had   happened   said   I couldn't
          tell my parents   it was   in a parking spot

of the pharmacy   finally   I think I let
          you   hold me   your or my pulse   throbbing
in my head   your or my tears   damp   on my neck

          or maybe

we   were still   waterless   and stiff

          your questions   like searchlights   scanned
                    the darkness
we scoured the car   and all the parking lot

that night   we could not   never did find –

                              my

          body

MAGIC SHOW

The trick, this time, is mine. No magician
   can saw me in half – without bunny or top hat
or spell cast, I have simply vanished.

Audience members, please.
   Thank you, thank you – yes,
the magic tonight was real.

I see you are amazed. I am the first person
   to shed the liability of corporeality.
I am sky-sprawled – ruled only by the crux

of purple dawn / iridescent night. No longer
   ruled by the liquid currency of bodies, I span milky
miles, bleeding only darkness. Surely you are surprised

that no one can mishold me, to say
   nothing of groping. I've said goodbye
to the most feckless of forms – the human hull.

Dear audience, you have not been deceived.
   I am manned only by atoms. I am thin as
a strand of dust, the naked eye cannot see me. No,

don't outstretch your hand – it cannot
   feel me. Call me the first woman to be
without a body. Its corrupt government is gone,

dissolved. Oh, silly body – it lacked claws,
   it wasn't fast, so I traded skeletal mass,
my tits, my ass. I gave way to galaxy – to gas, dust,

dark particle. I traded the heresy of flesh for solar
   power. The thrill of hallowed alchemy. I am
careless as comets. I am as small, as large as a fistful

of stars. Hydrogen and helium – oh! I am a happy
   nothing, like the black hole that is something.
I am mindless as lunar light. Unafraid of night.

The fence marks the secrets we kept, next
    to the rosebush, your barking dog, the soundtrack
of my growing older. Last night the city got smaller

while I slept. Your big laugh filled up the block, warming
    the yard we shared overlooking the harbour. As a teen,
I'd steal out under stars to smoke. The fence outlines

the secrets we kept. These last few years, you rarely left
    the house, curled into couch, curtains drawn to keep
thorns of light out. Last night the city got smaller while
    I slept.

I know, too, the charade of days, and the dents
    the body can leave in the bed – but this I never
said. The fence marks the secrets we kept, except

the time you let slip that'd you once saw my secret
    teenage smoking – said you wished you'd braved
the dark to join me. The city got smaller while

I slept. Does your dog know, or is he still waiting for
    you to come home? His bark hits me at the bone.
    The fence marks the secrets we kept. Last night,
the city got smaller while I slept.

You are a glass of water, spilling. Prostrate in bed, you send
a text: the ball of yarn emoji. Under it written: *my body.*
She doesn't respond. You mean to say *it is all soft knots*
from this not sleeping then evaporating into a fog of melatonin
& sleeping too far. Prescribed calm washes over you, a placid
baptism, heart a vacated crab shell. Coffee to wake back up
again. Limbs yawn to begin their brief lives. You covet cute dogs
in parks when taking your moods out for a walk. Slipping
back into sheets, you scroll the nomenclature of full moons.
Their names like quartz in the mouth: *Wolf Moon, Hunter's*
Moon, Strawberry Moon, Snow Moon, tonight's *Cold Moon.*
You ping-pong, shiver between wants. Hearing the front door,
recall your roommate, imagine her mass taking form over
the stove. Your envy traces how other bodies move. Do
anything today; a challenge for you to fail every hour. You
persist, another text: *are u there?* Curling toward the whirs & heat
the laptop makes, you step in and out of tears like a dress
that knows your shape. Her reply, blue glow of a text: *Yep*

HARVEST

In acrid sweetness, grapefruit is tang at tongue, acid
searing nervous finger cuts. Let me count the ways
I could have you, that I want to. The thrall of you
coming on, big as a season, ordinary as weather. Even
breakfast is suggestive: the rind is your skin, porous,
lost in limonene. The fruit's flesh ripe red, two halves open-
faced, its bitter blood staining the throat. The grapefruit was
man-made, orange via pomelo. We kneel, and burn, in cycles.
From the bowl, the fruit dreams of the country it came from.
Like lines of latitude, we lean into earth, never meeting.
The summer could love us. Meet me some July, in other
lives, another province, a bog lit by lupines. Let me touch
you underwater – at Middle Cove Beach, across Atlantic
algae sheets. We hurt, and are hurt, in cycles. The salt, they
say, is good for cuts. By midmonth, the capelin will roll in,
flush against shore, to spawn – the water so silver with fish
you can grab handfuls. Locals salt them for snacks,
or press their bodies into soil for better harvests.
Japanese markets covet capelin roe, the tiny beads
they call masago. It bleeds from their silver sides
as they beach. Almost no male survives the season.

Orbicular, dense with anthocyanins –
   the pigments that brush

their bodies in violet watercolour.
   Between fall's balsam fir & jack pine,

the blueberries beckon, only to dye
   each fingertip and stain the tongue

with their plum language –
   the damning testimony

of a private passion, like a secret lover
   whose touch leaves a bruise

on your lips. Slow bursts between
   teeth, their subdued sweetness –

a taste intangible as wind that blows
   through the body suddenly

and after leaves it heavier, like grief.
   Bushes of a hundred pea-sized stars,

these berries laid upon the branches
   by some capricious fairy who

craved more blue in the world.
   Fruit at the peak of its season is eager

for our mouths and we want to write
    lines like that down. But in these woods,

such well-worn tracks – your neural pathways
    braid urge, pain, reward. Buckets brim.

A morning's work of hillside picking
    that a midwinter night's dream painted

on your leaden eyelids. You fall from sleep
    like reclaiming your foot from a cliff's edge

too late. What's left: the ache of more yet to fill
    that you wake into. Days or hours pass,

September shifts to winter's blanched palate.
    Like the insistent prick of thorns

on exposed limb, your skin's familiar
    burn as though from stinging nettle.

That nag, nag, nagging feeling;
    a lust for picking – you dig, picking

skin as though to loosen a thought's grip,
    picking as though to return your body

to a former perfect order, picking
    until the sickening rush to pull

a string of it in one go, clean-off –
    while all the berries in every poem

you have not picked begin to spoil
   in faraway sun. From your window,

snow burdens every bough.

A place exists not imbued with
    such secrets, but not here, across

Atlantic marshes. Here, the stocky
    cave swallow speaks but not to mean.

It merely sings and is made slight by
    the lightness of its song. The pitcher plant

subsists on barren land – for this, we could
    call it tough, and evil twice as much, for the ways

in which it devours all those, winged or not,
    who fall into its cup. With nectar bribes

and slippery sides, the plant traps its errant
    victims and drinks them up. The kelp gull, too,

is cutthroat as a vulture in its hunt, and yet we
    think it tender because it mates for life.

Its bright yellow bill is red spotted – why, oh
    why, that one red dot? As if to mock our need

to know. The golden plover on the loam does
    not know, nor does he try to know. He doesn't

come here often, but this and other things are
    lost on him. He scans the land – part alive,

part dead, halfway dry, halfway wet – but not
   for precious messages. He simply seeks a bite to eat

to fight the cold. Across the marshes, he pecks
   at frozen berries in almost boredom, while

we are doomed to wonder whether
   his meal was tart or sweet.

ARCHIPELAGO

our rot of sweat & need   on blankets in Lafontaine
   we kissed & plucked   clouds to cool July heat

draped our reddening legs in the mist   lips
   honey / agave / maple   all things viscous / sweet

we fell like walls collapsing together   our bodies
   in the rubble   braided into knots so tight   it took

months for the dents   in my flesh
   to fade   each twilight drugged us purple

on Saturdays   like monks   we took   to the books
   spent Sunday mornings   nosing around

in poems   you waxed lyrical on angles
   of light that laid on the sill   Montreal's heat wave

in August   stained us with chlorophyll bruises
   in the smallness   of your room   hairs clung

like black snakes along wet necks   sweat pooling
   each place our skin met   our hearts running dry laps

not you no nothing sang   to me   except the fan
    the brand was Honeywell I think   a four-foot-tall hero

it could go / go / go   bet the whir of its motor
    even now   still reliably hums   to someone

every night   was the same for us   restless
    in your sheets   we needed   each other's backs

to double as screens   to conduct
    our dreams onto   and still

every morning   we woke up
    archipelago

Like a cherry blossom tree whose
blooms last a mere two weeks,

the Tunnock's Caramel Log is born
old, its texture somewhere between

sacramental bread and a wafer. Former
churchgoers know that this comparison is

favourable, because communion rolling around
meant – thank God – mass was nearly over.

Like the body of Christ, a Caramel Log has
an inspiring shelf life. No need, especially now,

to update its retro packaging: turns out
the best renovation is never changing.

This Log's layers of paper-thin wafer are enrobed
in silky milk chocolate – and the coconut? It's toasted.

The son of an Uddingston coffin maker,
Thomas Tunnock had loftier dreams of being

a baker. Wielding a strong Scottish name,
and uninhibited by class or gender,

he opened a bakery in 1890, and soon
went on to create a national treasure.

Like most nineteenth-century structures, the bakery
was bound to be destroyed by a fire once or twice.

It's fine. The whole of St John's, sure,
has burned down like a handful of times.

I don't know why. Maybe life back
then was simply more flammable.

In his failing health, Thomas's dying wish
was that his son, Archie, reopen the bakery –

which, in retrospect, probably wasn't fair,
but nothing new, really: parents tasking

children with fulfilling their unfulfilled dreams.
Some of these kids, like Archie, end up lucky:

members of a multi-million-pound empire, while
others end up broke after lifelong psychotherapy.

Like a Burns poem written in Scottish dialect can be,
the Log's inner workings seem sweet but are ultimately

indecipherable to me. It does have a single gram each
of protein and fibre, both essential, we know, for

a balanced diet – so don't dare call it empty calories
when there's nothing empty about it. You once took out

a bank loan to be able to afford dental work – but every
causation you stomached was worth it, because the Log

takes you right back to being sixteen – your first job
at Lawtons Drugs, gotten for you by your mom,

who worked as a secretary upstairs. (Let us reserve
usage of the term nepotism for occasions when it is

something others actually wanted, since Lawtons
was the kinda place that was always hiring.)

With the hum of fluorescent lights above,
the rumble of your belly below, you slouched

against the counter, pleasantly depersonalized
in a seafoam uniform. Between customers,

you'd sneak bites of a Caramel Log on cash
when you had hours still to go before your break.

Maybe your playground fun, too, was once
    some adult's nostalgic background track,

you think as the laughter of freed kids
    spills from a nearby recess bell.

Festive skeletons hang from front-yard
    branches, plastic hands emerging from

fake graves. You can't hear geese flying over,
    honking V-shaped order. On headphones,

you listen to playlists curated by algorithms
    who've learned the brush of your thumbs

by heart. To broach conversation again,
    you pull down thoughts, bobbing kites

from clouds, wrangle them into interpretable
    sounds. The basil needs dead-heading because

to flower uninhibitedly is to drain one's
    energy. Squirrels whet their teeth on the balcony,

mistaking composite for trees. It won't last.
    This structure will soon succumb to rot,

its visible wound symptomatic of a deeper cause.
    From your days, you've strained to sift out

preventable pains but now nights are such
   empty cups. The mice portend the advent

of cold weather by gnawing holes in pantry plastics.
   Like the Borrowers, squirrels exit leaf nests

when humans shift in beds. They've decapitated
   your black-eyed Susans. You tended their flowering

all spring, knowing they'd wilt come
   October frost. Like a lover whom your

hands urged to help grow, the return
   on investment for annuals is always low,

though both may prosper
   temporarily from your love.

ROMAN AUBADE

Wake up to get blistered or else destroyed by
A ruin. Naples ruined us on such gummy,
Buttery dough. *Take me now*, you slur from bed,
But my heart got lodged in a Keats poem – he sailed
South for a cure & died instead. In Rome we
Cried at deathbeds, getting sunburnt later on
The Spanish Steps. Trevi Fountain wishes made
No miracles of our tomato bodies.
Before Caravaggio's "Seven Acts of Mercy,"
The one at Pio Monte with the angel –
My first act: letting his light shafts rebuild me.
Babe, let us, too, bury the dead and refresh
The thirsty. But vacations end, I left you
In Campania – forgetting's an act of mercy.

ODE TO SLEEP

A miracle, to see me exiting my caved
   tomb – I always wake up new.

I have known deep and unshakeable
   slumbers, somnolence holier

than a church service. Being artless,
   in this skill alone I have confidence.

In my saddest seasons, sleep takes leave,
   but months later it'll return to love me

more deeply. A reprieve from thinking,
   a cure for moving and the disease of doing.

The trickle of a countryside brook
   never hastened the onset nor sharpened

the colour of my slumber. Lying
   amidst a city chorus of taxi horns

and stray lovemaking, sleep has equally
   laid into me. Even in view of Vesuvius,

my slumber went unperturbed,
   sleeping like a lamb against

her mother's wool, milk-full.
   Fear of monsters, imagined or real,

rarely kept me from sleep because
    I knew they couldn't harm me there.

A wound in dreams is scarless,
    you wake in sheets unmarred, while

good dreams can mercifully loan to you
    a loved one that death has stolen.

A lover's quarrel never delayed
    to that hallowed realm my ascent,

much to the chagrin of all those
    who've shared my bed. My barbs

easily relent to snores when that
    drunken drowsiness comes on,

and then no conversation or book
    seems worth pursuing any longer.

I've spent entire days moored on the couch,
    feared going out, thought once even of dying.

But others I've cherished every second of,
    beneath the stars in someone's arms, smiling.

All are ironed out in the same, terminal way:
    sleep baptizing my body with a cool, dark wave.

SFOGLIATELLA

Jesus   wasn't it good   eating
  sfogliatella for breakfast in Naples Square

cracking flakes   and their lemon sweet
  cut by coffee   on our balcony   that looked out

at a marble Dante   who seemed homesick
  his hand reaching out   for Florence

God waited for us   at every corner
  gilded crosses   and shrines in every shadow

me waiting still   for my higher power
  which I found in   the clotheslines that

stretched like arms   across streets
  garments waving   in slow motion

on Via Materdei   we got margheritas to go
  even worse   we got them at lunch   all of which

we soon   realized was a faux-pas
  we ate them   rolled up   still hot

ashamed on the sidewalk   the locals smiled at us
  like bad children   they still loved

on the way to Pompeii   the train was
  trembling   it rocked   back

and forth   like the restless toddler
    across from us   before we left of course

on stolen wifi   I had researched Vesuvius
    not all its eruptions   were ancient

I admit   my luv   I had intrusive thoughts
    about dying   but thought it noble that

I kept the conversation   banal and wanting
    So much of vacation   is faking it

to see   that mummified dog
    in plaster cast   his small body

left   at the door   chained up
    Pompeii was great   but it can really tank a day

I could not shake   the look on all
    their frozen faces   cruel voyeurism

of ruin   tourists laughing at dirty drawings
    and me sick   all through dinner

limbic system lit up   like a terrace at night
    my twin almonds spinning   in all their processing

You told me it was best   not to take ancient ruin
    so personally   I was thinking then

of saints   the mixed affect of churches
    an Italian trinity   of   God & carbs & coffee

All the while   Keats warm in my lap
    calling me   like a friend

I picked him up then   to read you an ode
    the one I love   about the bird

Hard to tell the thunder from
   another chorus of morning music

on Saint-Dominique – workers who
   move with saws, metal teeth sharp.

They have come to prune the tree that
   infringes on city property. A linden too big

for its britches. I am flesh where it is
   bark and yet, its departure marks me

still. Who knows how many rings
   its trunk holds, or how many tenants

it has loved, or loathed, or known.
   It lies now at a new angle upon the street,

and finches fly to it still – in ignorance,
   I wonder, or to underscore this grief?

Some bird, I hope, has the appropriate
   elegy. "Part of it lives on," they might sing,

(birds being not above trope) –
   "but it is a ghost of what it

once was," like a thumb
   cut off, nerves raw, exposed.

ICEBERG IN FERRYLAND

The landlocked arrive from all over
  just to take a gawk, parking their cars

amidst all the traffic pissing off
  Loop locals. They let their doors

hang ajar in mechanical awe, rushing out
  like you were about to dart off to visit

Edna Breen in The Pool, the Ferrylander
  who now keeps her drinks cold with your cubes.

Each eyeful is leaden in the chest, heavy like
  irrepressible memory. We know that you're neither

the first, nor the last. Icebergs visit every
  spring: the spawn of Baffin Island's glaciers,

or the estranged relations of Greenland's ice sheets,
  departing from cold origins, floating down

the coast, nudging into our coves as singular,
  white souvenirs. We covet your firm, taut sheen

and dearth of pores – secrets we could bottle
  and sell to Lancôme. Some watch you drip,

glisten through phone lenses, vying for
  the perfect angle, a picture to filter sublime

and post. The iceberg's agency is maybe that
   every photo proves inadequate. Its dimensions appear

unreal, as if painted, but unlike art, it is soluble –
   we love it most because the hours change it.

Your movements are slow, routine, and yet
   we stare, expecting you – like some great,

sleeping animal – to shift poses or awaken.
   Your slick, blue face glitters under sun

that spoiled us all April, stealing us
   more warm days for picking berries,

for chances at catching our narrowing
   allowance of cod. We have loved these boat rides,

have loved, too, the salt the sea licks
   skin with. And we never shut up about

the good weather – funny how each
   summer lately seems like the warmest

on record. Here we are, expecting,
   even hoping, that you will wilt away –

in a culture that loves to see
   a big celebrity degrade.

POWER'S STORE

In memory of Harold Power

The keeper of sweets at Power's Store
    arranged cans of SpaghettiOs in rows just

so. Even townies know. Harold's shop
    signals our car's arrival to Calvert

on Sundays, here where things
    are slow and worn. Road signs, these

are only guidelines. Shore locals
    like Gertie and Ellie and Aidan know.

In brown paper bags of candy,
    we dug our hands, trawling for sweets

like nets in the sea. We savoured
    the taxonomy of sweets: Swedish Berries'

identifying peaks, the exact feel of Jujubes
    between the teeth. Peppermint Nobs,

their soothing sugar-cool. Chocolate
    nonpareils: disks with rainbowed beads.

A star of the Southern Shore from
    the length of his store to The Beach,

Harold Power was the keeper of sweets,
  the confectionery king, dealing legal highs

in Caplin Bay from The Point to
  The North Side, to my sister & me.

The shop is long closed now. Remember
  that time he let us man the counter?

Even townies dream. We draw deep on Popeye
  cigarettes, hoping still, like children, for smoke.

MY FATHER'S FATHER

Daily you worked the fish: cut cods'
  heads, gut their bellies empty.

Clean, split, salt. Splay them across
  flakes on the stage down on The Beach

to dry, then repeat, stacking bodies
  tail to head, a rhythm my fingers never

knew to be able to forget. I have
  imagined the business of your hands,

shuffling dark rum back by boat
  from Saint-Pierre, palms coarse

from rope, wind, salt. You kept the Loop
  from going dry, and that was God's work,

surely. They call her a saint, your Viking-boned
  wife, whose adventures were confined

to the other side of the door. You ran a supply store
  over on the beach, bestowed on Caplin Bay

its molasses, cabbage – the great purveyor
  of sugar & flour. I have imagined the texture

of your smell: pipe smoke, sod, the steam
  off a boiled potato – like the heart of a Heaney poem,

in your utopia pre-existing the first
   smart phone. At my age, you moved

to Boston – but homesickness drove
   your schooner back to Gut Pond, back

to that mercurial province, where together
   you both raised cattle, twelve children, hens.

On today's date, your sterile summary of
   its hours: *Northwestern winds today. Cold. No fish.*

Your seaside home was an aging museum – shifting
   exhibits of dust, peeling wallpaper, crucifixes.

From the wall, you and Jesus in framed photos
   judged my sins of gluttony, sloth – gut-rot

from Swedish Fish, cartoon-watching
   the day away. Strange the way they all still

call you Daddy, while I'll never make
   a name for you. They fossilize the lilt

of your sayings, the mythology of your
   moods – the past is their candy.

Our birth-cries bookended a century.
   My cousin said she saw your ghost one night,

when the moon was sterling silk
   on the water. You'd been taking

a nap by the woodstove, and rose to look
    wordlessly at the ocean, just like you used to.

I HAVE NOT ALWAYS BEEN
AS CAREFUL AS I AM NOW

Once, I felt my time here was short. It became so.
Were mistakes just light I prevented
from entering me? Like my shadow,
their darkness projects in my shape.
Today I visited one of the houses we lived in
as children, stared from the sidewalk wondering
if a house has a memory. This evening,
I inhaled autumn beneath a balsam fir,
rubbed the dog's belly. Bravery is everywhere,
collecting itself like leaves in the space
between sidewalk and street. This evening
I helped a friend, at seventy-seven, sign up on a dating site,
three years following the passing of his wife.
How could anyone not call this, too, a life?

THE FEVER AND THE FRET

I. Rue Garnier

You stroll by past apartments
to see how you've been.

Like visiting old friends, you measure
lanyard change, the former lives

you lived with them. In stylized lowercase,
spring arrives, quietly making its statement,

the Plateau's magnolias cautious
to unfold, not wanting to upstage

human suffering. Their lilac-pink buds
badly contained like a hurtful secret

already ubiquitous in every street.
Blooms born old, they rarely make it

to summer solstice. Grown women call their
mothers too often, whose voices are butter again.

❦

The front yard on Garnier, where
into earth you invested perennial ferns,

hands forcing permanence where
it didn't belong. In the damp kitchen

where silverfish fed on oat dust
and stained dish linens, he taught you,

at twenty-one, how to hold a knife properly.
Along the soft of your forearms,

hot cookie sheet scars from waitress
dreams of being a pastry chef star.

Reams of croissant dough laminated
inseparably: the nature of memory.

August sun stamping us, Pimm's cups
and Benson & Hedges for lunch,

back porch summer. Like plotting constellations,
you taught him aunt and uncle names, jabbing air

to illustrate your family's extending web
while he topped up drink after drink.

More Hendrick's, more cigarettes
to soothe sunburns & boredom until –

you came to. Body heat-stroked, shaking
limbs. Legs like pool noodles, heels dangling

over the icy bath he drew for you. How nice
to lie in a bathroom you could call your own.

In the mirror, your lips
still a little blue.

Come spring, red-squared students
marched the street, banged pots & pans

outside the window, exposing
the stale quiet of that bedroom.

Your quickening breath
fogged the glass, hopeful.

Like a cloud blocking
the moon, he cold-shouldered

their clang and politic
with neon foam earplugs.

At the restaurant where you met him,
you used to meet in secrecy to kiss

in the cilantro-scented chill
of the walk-in fridge.

Your first date: dinner at Brasserie T,
then The xx at Salle Wilfrid-Pelletier.

You tasted tartare twice:
nerves & booze loosened

your dinner onto his shoes
as he kissed you goodnight.

Two years later, boxes of your
stuff thrown onto the sidewalk.

You paid rent but crashed
in Rebecca and Mario's office

in Parc Ex, sucked salt from almonds
for supper, spat them out. Took bites

from blocks of cheese, ate spoonfuls
of hummus, called this sustenance.

Set reminders on your phone
to drink water, touched bony knees,

elbows & cheeks where
flesh used to be.

II. Avenue Querbes

Crossing the first night alone on
the way to their Querbes apartment,

your body dilated, the smallness
of life smashed into a thousand

shimmering sidewalk shards. You harnessed them
to the stars above, grew larger than yourself.

When the going gets tough,
the tough get going,

your mother's platitudes warm
and generic like a hotel blanket.

Your only furniture, suitcases of
books, made the taxi bottom-heavy.

You wrote an end-of-term paper
on Sonnet 130, critiquing idealization

in romance while spooning a tissue box
on a pull-out couch, profs & dep owners

& grocery store clerks all brutally incognizant
of how heavy it is to carry a broken heart.

As the metre's red digits morphed,
you fantasized about the car crashing

to match internal disaster. Suddenly
you had no one to text you *good morning*,

unable to remember how a day
ended or started. At the bottom

of Gmail's crypt, you find extant decade-old
drafts addressed to him. A ghostly chorus

of *sorry, sorry, sorry.* That pain is ore,
glittering at the bottom of a lake,

finally too far down
to reach now.

III. Avenue St-Marc

The scent of chicken curry from Thali
hangs over the gravel stretch between

Saint-Catherine and de Maisonneuve, spiking
appetites. The building's been demolished,

its peculiar absence like the street's missing
tooth. You lived there, four roommates, a pug.

In curtain seams and box springs,
the room's bed bugs nested & multiplied.

Chain-smoking in bed, you used to watch
Montréalais with bottles of wine in tow,

scurrying hand in hand beneath the window.
You were always waiting for life, in some formalized way,

to begin. Getting or growing out bangs, missing
garbage day – turns out that, too, was living.

IV. *Rue Clark*

Into empty stomachs, a bottle each
of ten-dollar shimmering pink

from the SAQ on Pine Avenue
for you & the friend who's in town.

How to convince her that life here
has a film-like glimmer?

St-Laurent strewn with the promise
of espresso & croissants, every park bopping

like the entire city perpetually has
the next day off from work.

Tomorrow's Osheaga, but today
is Tam-Tams. Over bike shorts,

you sport a floral A-line skirt, pair it
with plastic earrings, cat-eye liner, a fedora.

Fingerprints on her Android's camera lens make
photos from that August day appropriately hazy.

Booze sanded down the edges of every
hour. Azure hues of noon replaced

by twilight, then spell of midnight.
From shitty phone speakers, we play

High Violet. Her fingers percuss. You love
her drumming. At Parc Jeanne-Mance,

time turned liquid like Heraclitus's river,
waters coursing with Mateus sparkling rosé.

Each step: strawberry-sweet, spinning pink,
different. At our backs, mountain fireflies

pricked the air with their bioluminescence,
just another phenomenon cheapened

by scientific explanation: oxygen combined
with calcium, ATP, luciferin.

Fireflies, you drunkenly proclaim, merit
another century of awed poetic dedication.

At Mont-Royal's peak, the LED-cross
erected first in wood and nail

by Paul de Chomedey de Maisonneuve, in ode
to the Virgin Mary whose hands in 1642

stalled waters from flooding the colony. At the picnic
table, a shivery blast of dopamine from inhaling

the pack's last menthol cigarette. The memory
narrows then, into minted-black.

The morning after, you vomit, then shower.
Like the unique intensity of each new crush,

every hangover feels freshly brutal.
Your festival outfit: cognac booties

with a thrifted dress, chambray & stripes.
In a group of four, we ride metro cars

through stale-air tunnels to Osheaga,
to see Snoop Dogg, Kathleen Edwards,

Sigur Rós, the standard catch-all lineup.
At various stops across orange & yellow metro lines,

the popsicle returns, unprompted as memory –
bodiless, a slick, purple syrup.

In a compact mirror, you reapply MAC's
Russian Red lipstick before bailing on Osheaga

to crawl into bed. Back at the triplex
on Rue Clark, your stomach's dial, again

and again, aches empty. At midnight,
a craving from nowhere: breakfast the way

your dad served it in the nineties, a glass of SunnyD,
white bread toasted, margarine-soaked, sliced

into soldiers, served with
a boiled egg's sunrise yolk.

V. *Rue Saint-Dominique*

At the rear entrance of Segal's, waves
of delivery trucks park & depart.

They unload cargo onto the dock: cases
of kombucha, tempeh, nutritional yeast.

You would sweat over mop buckets nearby,
free yoga in exchange for your labour

at the studio where a teacher would
adjust your angles in Triangle Pose.

You wanted to wash off the dirt of his palms after
learning he tries to fuck all the program's volunteers.

The stench of bacalhau in crates
fills the store, nostalgia anvil

onto chest: the salt cod smell
of your coastal childhood kitchen.

"Two lines, people!" Murphy hollers.
His frugal patrons obey and divide.

At a Rue William loft party, someone hands you
a travelled copy of *A New Earth* by Eckhart Tolle.

Cool, thanks, you say. *Just the other day,
I was trying to awaken my life's purpose.*

Usually you are too hungover, nailing
blankets over windows in lieu of curtains.

It's 2013 and C. is trying polyamory –
which she confesses in her case means

that *my partner has sex with everyone while
I secretly hope he'll revert to monogamy.*

In a crowded stairway, en route
to the rooftop where a circus performer is

set to test homemade fireworks, someone
in a bear tuque playing ukulele pauses their song

to extend a palm of MDMA. You decline, not
impiously. Back at the loft, everyone dances in

stately undress to Flume and What So Not, heads
haloed by amphetamines, caressing each other's skin,

staying up all night but no one staying
hard, while warm mason jar-gin

sinks you deeper into the couch,
alcohol and anxiety like elevator doors

coming together to trap you
inside yourself.

In Little Portugal, retirees lounging on porches watch
Gen Z trends come and go in bored disapproval.

You leave the house with the phone's battery
at 2 per cent: is this living life on the edge?

You refresh your website
to see if you're somebody yet.

September's crunch of zapped leaves, the missing
blare along St-Laurent of McGill's frosh week.

You worked at a café here that sells
ethically sourced arabica beans.

During breaks, you'd squeeze in grad school reading:
Rankine pdfs on a shattered iPhone screen.

You miss the tactile mechanics: dunking
steam wands into pitchers, the squeal of its heat

as it churned milk fats to microfoam. From
all angles, you were being watched – panoptic.

Some customers came for a latte;
others, the spectacle of personality.

Your shift mate: a DJ who recently
performed in Berlin. You said: *I'm not really anything*.

You debt began to deepen – more discernible
with age, like inherited crow's feet.

The wage, eleven dollars and a quarter per hour was like
mending a flooding boat's hole with paper towel.

Bloom: the term for hot water hitting freshly ground coffee,
the caramel-coloured puff of released carbon dioxide.

Bloom: the way anxiety balloons
black and racking into the body.

VI. *Avenue de Normanville*

Across Avenue du Parc, the 80 floats by,
weightless, no one aboard to push *Arrêt*.

Montreal grows older in anachronisms:
the yeasty waft of sourdough loaves

breaking from windows. Restless neighbours
prematurely break in balconies with blankets,

mugs of tea. You send calls to voicemail,
stare searchingly at strangers, storm ruelles

blasting new Fiona Apple. The kitchen ficus turns
pale, drops its leaves, wordless in its mortal grief.

Parc La Fontaine's pond is drained,
empty save for a few Pabst cans,

gravy-stained take-out containers
from La Banquise – so post-lapsarian.

Remembrance of picnics past. Every
patch of earth, a spot where your blanket

has flattened grass. Remember summer of '14
with the Australians? If it rained, we picnicked

indoors, eating salad with tahini-sesame
dressing in their Rue Clark living room.

Sangria was a way to seem dignified
while fortifying wine with Cointreau.

The minted mango at the bottom
of those boozy cups alone would

knock your head off. Fond memories,
if only you could remember them.

SPVM officers on bikes ticketed us
for drinking dépanneur wine

long into midnight, tipping the last
of Toro Loco into our mouths,

legs wobbly when we finally stood up
to Bixi to watch a band we didn't

know yet play at L'Escogriffe.

In May, a frost warning
and snowfall. You listen

to productivity podcasts
with tidal focus, watch

Dutch art history videos,
missing what the scholar dubs

essential knowledge, scroll
through an article that brags

during plague quarantine, *King Lear*
was written. By whom, even?

New window: clickbait authorship theories –
The Atlantic's "Was Shakespeare a Woman?"

You weave in and out of tabs
of sonnets like rooms,

116, then 15 (a 3.8 star
Google rating), then search

shakespeare sonnet love sickness for the one
you always forget: sonnet 147, gleaming

on an Acer laptop screen in Arial font,
webcam washi-taped to keep

the Dark Lady trapped inside from
looking out. Beneath glass in Hampstead,

visitors can see Keats's annotations on
Shakespeare's plays – or was it *Paradise Lost*?

You stood above the bed where
his friend Charles Brown watched

Keats cough onto a pillow and
mutter: *That is blood from my mouth*.

To friends on postcards, you jokingly
wondered: how often did Keats get off?

The unspoken bodily facts
of his proto-Victorian life:

did Keats die in Rome untouched, while
Shelley & Byron spread ass across Europe?

This spring, the Spanish Steps
feel little footfall. Though its waters

still trickle, few coins are tossed
into the Trevi Fountain. Wishes

go ungranted. On its 2773rd birthday, Rome
has no party. *Dolce far niente* has been spoiled.

An idle country daydreams
its risanamento.

To Fanny Brawne in a letter two hundred Marches ago,
Keats writes: *I shall kiss your name and mine*

where your Lips have been – Lips! why
should a poor prisoner as I am

talk about such things. On your bookshelf,
a daisy pressed between "Lamia" pages,

plucked from his front yard, where in
sickness he'd ogle Fanny beneath his window:

You shall have a pleasant walk to day. I shall
follow you with my eyes over the Heath.

Tonight you can type the title
of any poem into Firefox. Instead,

you stream *Reality Bites*. A past teenage self
falls for Troy Dyer in a diner reading *Being and Time*.

You consider buying a dress on eBay
to slip into Winona Ryder from the nineties.

Projected shipping time from Beijing is five weeks,
the time it took Keats to travel from London

to Naples by boat in 1820. But by June,
you'll want Clementine's Blue Ruin hair,

though you're just as much Joel & most
of all Mary, quoting Pope stoned.

To A. you text the three tercets
of "Poet's Work" by Niedecker,

followed by the crying-laughter
emoji. *No layoff from this condensery.*

Elizabeth lists the birds who've returned
to your ruelle's elms. In glimpses: the black-blue

plumage of starlings. Eugene Schieffelin, in
1890, released sixty starlings into Central Park.

His goal: to bring the birds of Shakespeare's plays
to North America – but the species became invasive.

E. took an undergraduate ornithology course;
there are none she does not know.

Your eyes hold them but your mouth can't let them
go, since your degrees only taught you birds via poems.

On headphones, you play "Ode to a Nightingale
(British accent)," lying between equidistant trees

in Parc Père-Marquette, the site of a former
quarry, filled and manicured to football green.

Where men once mined limestone for houses,
a teenager bent over bleachers rolls a joint,

though now the government sells its own THC,
pre-rolled bats in plastic tubes from the SQDC.

Developers sought to solicit new
tenants to Petite-Patrie in 1890, citing

*the pleasures of country life, clean air,
tranquility, far from the noise.*

The borough mayor now wants
to kill traffic, form *super blocks* à la

Barcelona to stave off *suburbanites
crossing through the city* on side streets.

Beneath nearby golden arches,
unbroken rounds of fryer baskets

are lifted from oily baths dense
with French fries, and dutifully salted.

The scent of Happy Meals® drenches the park,
childhood drive-through Fridays coat your mouth.

Employees snap hairnets
over beards and braids,

haul on smokes behind the dumpster
during breaks and the shift change.

The temperature climbs to thirty-five. Precarious
protrusions from sills, AC units rattle

into rickety overdrive. Layers of skin
seem to slough off in sweat, your body

getting thinner like a candle
beneath its hot, tiny ember.

Humid air like a towel
against your mouth,

you breathe shallow. Former addicts
fantasize about regularity, routine,

while the disciplined daydream of disorder,
the courage to disappoint a friend.

Summer is a blood orange
we peel back and eat, sweeter

thanks to our new little freedoms.
A purported mutation between pomelo

and tangerine, blood oranges are dyed
by anthocyanins. Tonight you float along

Boulevard Rosemont, phone between
shoulder & ear, company from the voice

of Rebecca and the sky's magenta.
As if on cue, because all feels hopeless,

the city pulls back the curtain
on what you'd miss. Back home,

the monstera's leaves begin to emerge,
tight little scrolls. You sit alone

in the kitchen's southwest light,
and dream of their unfolding.

I COME HOME TO REMEMBER
WHY I HAVE TO LEAVE AGAIN

Geometric glacial fissures, March's warmth
  breaking ice like a spoon cracking crème brûlée.
Below, the blue-marbled cream of lake water.
  Loons, unfazed by weather's whims but tuned
to the clock of seasons, know exactly where
  to nest, reclaiming former haunts in yellow-green
mossy backends. I come home to remember
  why I have to leave again.

The loon's memory is practical, physical – returning
  often to the same mating sites, the same lakes,
ponds. Some say they are faithful more to a location
  than to last year's mate. Apartment leases in this country,
every day, are broken or sworn. In the spirit of spring, I keep
  trying to begin again   but old browser cache re-emerges
in new laptops. Remembered passwords, addresses auto-filled.
  I knew where to go. I had no mind of my own.

A hometown is a data centre where the past
  is stored. The loon's celebrity eludes him,
his silhouette graces every dollar traded for cases
  of hollow beer bottles. His call from afar is lonely,
doleful. But like listening to Joni's *Blue*, sad in a way
  that lightens your alone. Take a breath, a step, another
breath, step. Steady now. The world is yet full of places
  where you are unknown.

In morning mist, birds begin their ministry.
  (Always beginning, as if not existing until

they are heard or seen.) The rubber tread
  of the bike's front wheel, like a horse,

draws my weight forward. Goldman, Notkin,
  Brownstein read the rows of headstones.

Against the bike's frame, I lean into relief, an instant
  of forgetting – only to remember again, a jolt:

your love is a country
  that I barred myself from.

The formerly faithful go nowhere on Sundays,
  yet I found myself at these gates, standing in all

my faith, in search of a man whose songs were
  lifelines on lovelorn teenage nights.

This decade-long downward tilt of my neck:
  eyes on my phone, tracking the blue angular snake

that leads to Cohen's grave. This device in my palm,
  its reassuring weight, seems suddenly out of place.

Feels like I should be holding paper, or vellum,
  or papyrus, or something as old itself as death.

Still, I cannot resist a picture in digital pixels:
   a bough framing grey sky, tulips testing earth,

headstones outlined by mountain – resigning
   myself to the Faustian bargain. I am all animal pain,

primal: my throat could open to howl at clouds,
   but a force beyond bones keeps me going.

A masked family in black enters. I leave but
   remain outside – unable to stand still, or move.

By the memory of freedom, along streets
and avenues, we are taunted. Nothing sweet is
in season yet, but mouths ache, hungry. Reveries
of strawberries, soft & wet, pooling in stained
cartons. What is relief? That we could touch the way
a rainstorm fails to drench July afternoon heat.
All winter, alone, I roamed forsaken sidewalks.
Frost misted window corners. Hydrangeas shivered
beneath snow. Loneliness hardened the world, dyeing
fingertips blue. A kiss was like Andromeda – such a bright,
faraway thing. But the amaryllis in my throat did not die;
its bulb went dormant. What is longing? That I cannot
picture the distance between two bodies ever closing. Many
nights of my life I worshipped stars, splayed into grass,
forgetting where the ground was. What is love? That I circled,
again and again, back to the altar of myself. Your name is
a hundred green buds waking the maple trees. April rays
are a fever in me, skin crimsoning. Courage is dreaming
your fingers in every place the sun cannot reach.

amid an ocean breeze   with weary hands   someone I loved
handed a stone   to me   said   *I cannot lift this*
I mistook it   for a gift   so I carried   the stone
everywhere   with me   into parties   convenience stores
even   into bed   as someone rolled   against my body
my skin   grew mineral   leaden tongue   shoulders sagging
with weight   lovers asked *how did you come to carry   a thing
so heavy*   well   I was the stone   and it was me   our dark
lives cut   from the same quarry   in some   shadowy cave
a miner had   absolved us   of our obscurity   together
we enjoyed   metallic   of nighttime   rainfall   on lakes
the dawn after   a full moon   how   could I   give up
something   made of someone   who   loved me
the stone had been   passed down   so long   my hands
were shaped   to hold   its ache   my arms born   to bear
this weight   some things   just   *are*   the rattle of trees
make manifest   the wind's shape   do you know anything
at all   about fate   some nights   I dreamt   that I lost it
forgot it on   some park bench   or metro car   with wet eyes
I'd awaken   no longer sure how   to relate   to the world
unable   to move   I'd stay   all day   ashen in bed
curled against   its cold mass   until the months   I grew
too sick   to eat   losing sinew   white hair falling
to earth   like snow   wrists brittle   I could   barely lift
myself so   I dragged   my body   to the tip   of the coast
so long   had I carried it   so long   had I called it   home
by that late hour   in my life   I did not fear goodbyes so
with my last   thin-boned powers   I hugged   the stone close
I shut   my eyes   at the edge   held   my breath   but

instead   I let   the stone   go   it fell   down
and   down   and   down   and   down   until
it crashed   against the waves   then   gravity dragged it
to the dark floor   of the sea   and I   hauled myself   all
the way   home   with the muscle   the stone   had
left behind in me   lately   I have been   learning
how to live   I am   learning   what   love is
I do not   think about   the stone   every
day   every   hour   anymore   but   please
do not   call me   free

PURPLE BALLOONS

We can't figure it out: on countless
    porches of Shea Heights houses,

bobbing in the breeze, purple balloons –
    tied to posts and windows.

With Tims in the truck's cupholders,
    we tourist around our own town.

Outside the Village Mall, six Metrobuses are
    stationed – dormant horses before the races.

A roommate who regularly stole my groceries
    once told me, *Life's not a spectator sport, dude.*

We park, laconic, to watch the Atlantic
    breaking against Petty Harbour's rocky coast.

Stealing a drive in the middle of remote work
    deadlines, we shirk Teams and Zoom screens

where colleagues' heads bob in squares,
    strained water cooler talk, routers glitching.

In lieu of gallery paintings, we now closely
    examine your boss's use of punctuation.

I like the mist. I like the day's 144p quality,
    the dearth of ads. No influencers around

to sell me a Casper mattress or HelloFresh subscription
　　here where the ocean meets the continental shelf.

Besides, I've redeemed those discount codes,
　　and cannot redeem them again. I've tried, utterly

lacking the ingenuity to conceive of meals
　　and longing to visit the rolling country of sleep.

What's the harm in targeted ads
　　if we're being sold something

we already want? As if desire weren't
　　born in us by the consummation

of a lack and external cause. Some days I move,
　　but others I just float, watching life happen

in the distance from a dingy boat. You,
　　the amateur physicist, attempt to explain

ocean spray, its pyrotechnics. *I should look it up,*
　　I say – but don't. To call this coastal visit

an escape would be untrue. Sickness – or
　　the news – just follow you. From your jeans:

ping. An email coming in. At Mary Lou's,
　　the clerk says the balloons are for a kid

from the neighbourhood. She died of a rare
　　disease that she battled all her short life.

On the hushed route home, the houses we
    again drive past, every balloon different now,

a part of the procession – her funeral mass.
    When a gust cuts one loose on Linegar,

the balloon tumbles into air like a dog freed
    from its leash. Up, and up, and up it goes,

a purple conspirator with wind and flight.

"Ode to McCain's Deep'n Delicious Cake" quotes lines from Robert Frost, "Nothing Gold Can Stay," in *North of Boston* (New York: Signet Classics, 2001).

"Iceberg in Ferryland" references the iceberg from April 2017, and details from "'Pretty amazing' to see your house on an international stamp, says N.L. family," *CBC News*, 19 January 2019.

"The Fever and the Fret" makes reference to, or sources material from, the following articles: Katherine Wilton, "The Cross on Mount Royal: A Storied History, " *Montreal Gazette*, 6 January 2015; Daniel Pollack-Pelzner, "Shakespeare Wrote His Best Works During a Plague," *The Atlantic*, 14 March 2020; Elizabeth Winkler, "Was Shakespeare a Woman?," *The Atlantic*, June 2019; and Jason Horowitz, "Rome Has Been Sacked, Conquered and Abandoned. Now It's the Pandemic's Turn," *The New York Times*, 1 May 2020. The (potentially apocryphal) anecdote regarding Eugene Schieffelin is referenced from Jane O'Brien, "The birds of Shakespeare cause US trouble," *BBC News*, 24 April 2014.

The poem contains lines from Lorine Niedecker, "A Poet's Work," in *Collected Works* (Berkeley: University of California Press, 2002), and Brendan Kelly, "Rosemont has new plan to try to push traffic off of side streets," *Montreal Gazette*, 8 May 2020. The poem also contains lines from John Keats's personal letters from 29 February 1820 and 1 March 1820 (John Barnard, ed., *Selected Letters*

[London: Penguin Books, 2014]). Biographical details relating to Keats were sourced from Stanley Plumly, *Posthumous Keats: A Personal Biography* (New York: W.W. Norton, 2009).

Clementine, Joel, and Mary are characters from Michel Gondry's *Eternal Sunshine of the Spotless Mind* (Focus Features, 2004). I also make reference to Martin Harris, "'Ode to a Nightingale,' John Keats (British accent)," YouTube, 17 April 2014.

ACKNOWLEDGMENTS

Thank you to all the readers, editors, and judges who published or acknowledged my work in some way. A selection of these poems appeared in *Arc Poetry Magazine*, *The Malahat Review*, *The Antigonish Review*, *Room Magazine*, *Riddle Fence*, *subTerrain*, *Newfoundland Quarterly*, *Grain Magazine*, *Canthius*, *Southword Journal*, and *Prairie Fire*. Parts of this collection were shortlisted or longlisted in the following contests: The 2020 Montreal International Poetry Prize; *Arc*'s 2020 Poem of the Year contest, *Room*'s 2020 Poetry Contest, *The Malahat Review*'s 2020 Far Horizons Award and 2020 Open Season Award, the 2019 CBC Poetry Prize, *Riddle Fence*'s 2021 Poetry Contest, *subTerrain*'s 2021 Lush Triumphant Award, and *The Antigonish Review*'s 2020 Great Blue Heron Contest. For their financial support which made this book possible, thanks to The Canada Council for the Arts, and the grantors of the Brenda Mackie Artist Award at the Banff Centre for the Arts and Creativity.

Thanks to the Banff Centre for allowing me to work on this manuscript for a month in the Rockies, and for giving me an ID card that said "Artist" on it. Thanks to all the Banff mentors, especially Karen Solie and Aisha Sasha John, for being casual founts of wisdom and inspiration. Thank you to the brilliant writers I met at Banff who taught and influenced me, too.

Thanks to those of my graduate cohort at Concordia who read my work deeply and made it stronger. Thank you to all the Concordia professors who taught me literature and made it feel vibrant; I learned something valuable from every one of you. Thanks to my grade nine Language Arts teacher, Ms Lester, who said my poem about the ocean was good and started all this. Thank you to Stephanie Bolster – a sharp, warm, and generous mentor whose insight guided many of these poems to better ends, and whose advice I continue to cherish and benefit from.

Thank you to my editor, Allan Hepburn, who finessed these poems in their final stages. Thank you to Penelope, who enthusiastically received the first drafts of all these poems and treated them with a scrupulous kind of care.

Thank you to all my loved ones – my friends, my partner, my family – who helped me get here.